Hand-Dipped Candles

excerpted from *The Candlemaker's Companion* **by Betty Oppenheimer**

CONTENTS

Introduction

Humans have used light to lengthen and brighten their days for 15,000 years. Hollowed-out stones filled with animal fat and used as lamps were among the earliest light sources. Modern-day oil lamps work in much the same way, with a wick pulling fuel up to a flame. Early methods of torch lighting involved soaking papyrus, flax, or other fibers in resins, pitch, or natural oils and burning them as torches. This technique progressed to the use of twisted fibers dipped in various combustible substances that remain solid at room temperature. These dipped fibers were early versions of candles.

A candle is a body of tallow, wax, or other fatty material formed around a wick and used for a portable light. In other words, a candle is a solid chunk of fuel wrapped around a wick. A candle works because the wick burns and melts the solid fuel into a liquid, which is transported by capillary action ("wicked") to the flame, which vaporizes the fuel and burns it off.

Dipping is one of the oldest methods of candlemaking and one of the most hands-on. It is the process of building up layers of wax on a wick. The dipping process naturally creates tapers. I remember as a child watching in fascination as the women of Colonial Williamsburg dipped candles methodically and described the skill as one of the many tasks of a homemaker in early America. In addition to making the candles, women collected animal fats or berries and possibly raised bees to get the wax they needed. Today, most dipped candles are made of paraffin or beeswax or a blend of the two. Dipping harkens back to the early "rush dips," long, fired grasses that were dipped into grease and used like torches.

A Brief History of Candles

It is hard to imagine the world of early candlelight, with its wide variety of materials, the hundreds of years with few or no technological breakthroughs, and the fact that the match (that little item we take for granted every day) was not invented until 1827!

Early candles were made of vegetable waxes produced from plants such as bayberries, candelilla leaves, candletree bark, esparto grass, and various varieties of palm leaves such as carnauba and ouricury. They were also made of animal tissue and secretions, such as spermaceti (whale oil), ambergris, and beeswax (insect secretions). Sometimes entire animals such as the stormy petrel and the candlefish of the Pacific Northwest were threaded with a wick and burned as candles. Tallow candles were made of sheep, cow, or pig fat. All these candles were rather crude, time-consuming to make, smoky, and smelly.

Of the two kinds of candle fuel, beeswax was considered the better product, as it burned cleaner than tallow and had a lovely odor compared to tallow's rancid, smoky burn. Being scarce, beeswax was much more expensive. Only churches and the wealthy could afford beeswax candles. In fact, church rules insisted on beeswax candles because of the belief that bees were blessed by the Almighty. It was ordered that Mass be performed even during the day by the light of wax made by bees, as they represented spiritual joy.

Early chandlers dipped wicks into melted wax or poured wax over wicks repeatedly until a thick coating built up. In the 15th century wooden molds were developed, but they could not be used for beeswax because it was too sticky to release from wooden surfaces. The molded candlemaking method did make the process of forming tallow candles much easier, however, and tallow candles became more available and affordable. Still, candles burned quickly and their wicks had to be continuously trimmed (originally called snuffing) to prevent smoking.

By the 17th century, European state edicts controlled the weight, size, and cost of candles. In 1709, an act of the English Parliament banned the making of candles at home unless a license was purchased and a tax paid. Rushlights, made by dipping rushes or reeds in suet, were excluded from the tax and became the cheapest form of lighting. But, surprisingly, many peasants still bought the more expensive candles because their poverty meant little meat — and little suet — in their diet.

The 19th century finally brought with it a burst of new discoveries and inventions that revolutionized the candle industry and made lighting available to all. In the early- to mid-19th century, a process was developed to refine tallow with alkali and sulfuric acid.

The result was a product called stearin. Stearin is harder and burns longer than unrefined tallows. This breakthrough meant tallow candles could be made without the usual smoke and rancid odor. Stearins were also derived from palm oils, so vegetable waxes as well as animal fats could be used to make candles.

Also in the 19th century, a method was developed for braiding wick fibers. This caused them to bend over and away from a candle's flame, where they would burn to ash and eliminate the need for the constant snuffing, or trimming, of a candle's wick. In addition, chemical treatments were developed for wick fibers that made them less flammable, so candles would burn longer and more efficiently.

Matches, which were invented in 1827 using poisonous phosphorus, improved by the end of the century, eliminating the need for sparking with flint, steel, and tinder, or for keeping a fire burning 24 hours a day.

But probably most important of all, paraffin was refined from oil around 1850, making petroleum-based candles possible. The combination of paraffin, which burns cleanly and without odor, and stearins, which harden soft paraffin, with new wick technologies developed in the 19th century, revolutionized the candle industry, giving us the tools and materials we still use for candle manufacturing.

While candlemaking materials improved, however, kerosene became popular as a less expensive and readily available replacement for whale oil lamp fuel. When this happened, oil lamps became the preferred source of artificial light. So even though candles improved in the 19th century, they never held as important a position as they did when they were the only available light source. In fact, 20th-century sales of candles are on a par with late-19th-century sales.

Nowadays, candles are used predominantly for romantic atmosphere, during electrical outages, and in spiritual quests and religious rituals. We share this with our 19th-century relatives — we never stopped using candles, even after we no longer needed them!

Candlemaking Basics

To understand how to dip candles, you must first understand a few key concepts about how candles burn, and what supplies are required to make them burn well. A candle flame burns because of the two main ingredients: fuel and wick. When you light a candle, the wick catches fire and that fire heats to melting a small pool of wax just below the flame. The wick draws up that liquid wax to feed the flame, and the wick burns away at the top. In a good candle, the fuel (wax) burns more quickly than the wick does.

When you're burning your candles, watch the wick and flame in order to determine whether you have achieved good combustion. A candle that is burning well will have a 1- to 2-inch, steadily burning flame. The wick should bend over at approximately 90 degrees or stick straight up into the oxidation zone at the top of the flame so that the tip is almost to the edge of the flame and can burn to ash. The wax should form a liquid pool surrounding the wick — not so big as to spill over but not so dry that the wick has no liquid to pull up.

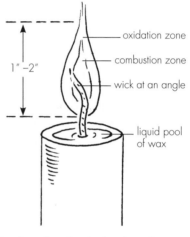

Good combustion is the sign of a well-made candle.

All about the Wick

The relationship of the wick to the wax, in terms of burn rate, is what determines whether a candle will burn well — or at all.

Before the invention of braided, mordanted wick, a variety of twisted fibers were used to carry the flame of a candle. Since they did not curl predictably — modern wicks bend over an exact 90 degrees — the wick stayed in the hottest part of the combustion zone and smoked as it carbonized.

Now, a wick is a braided (plaited) bundle of cotton threads, or plies, that has been mordanted, or pickled in a chemical solution. The mordant, or pickling, used on a wick is essentially a fire-retardant solution. It sounds strange to say a candle wick is treated to retard burning, but a candle's fuel (wax) should burn before the wick does so the wick can act as a fuel delivery system between the wax and the flame. The mordant causes the wick to burn more slowly and to decompose fully when it is exhausted.

People burning candles before the various innovations of the 19th century had to "snuff" them frequently. Snuffing means snipping off the wick to ½ inch, to prevent smoking.

Braiding plays an important role in the burning characteristics of a wick. The spaces between the braided plies allow more air into the combustion zone than would a nonbraided cord. In addition, braiding forces the wick to bend as it burns, which means the tip of the wick moves out of the combustion zone, where it can burn off completely.

To burn a candle properly, trim the wick to within ¼ inch of the wax surface before lighting. This cuts down on the excess carbon that builds up on the wick and prevents the candle's flame from becoming too big.

It is difficult to pinpoint exactly what wick you should use for a candle, but there are general guidelines you can follow. Most commonly available candlemaking supplies will indicate which wick is recommended for the wax and type of candle you are making. For example, a wick package will say, "Use this wick for all 1½-inch-diameter candles." This is a good place to start, but be aware that your choice of wax may have as much impact on the success of a candle as the choice of a wick for a particular-size candle.

Suppliers of wick material usually classify candles by diameter: for example, extra small (0–1), small (1–2 inches), and medium (2–3 inches). Within these size guidelines, certain types of wick work better with certain candle shapes and types of wax.

Wicks for dipped candles are usually flat-braided or square-braided. Most suppliers' labels indicate the wick's best use, but this information will give you some familiarity with the choices.

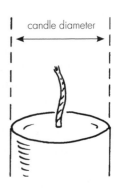

Types of Wax

Wax is the fuel that burns in the flame of a candle. Generally speaking, candle wax can be liquefied between 100°F and 200°F and is solid at room temperature. There are waxes from animal, vegetable, and mineral (petroleum) sources. Commercially refined waxes are used in food and pharmaceutical

Candle diameter plays an important role in wick selection.

Which Wick?

There are three general types of wicks to choose from for candle-making. For tapers, flat braid and square braid are the two best choices. Cored wicks, which have a paper, cotton, zinc, or lead core, work best with container candles.

Flat Braid

This is basically what it sounds like — a three-strand braid made of many plies per strand. Flat-braided wick is referred to by the number of plies in the wick, so the larger the number, the larger the wick. Common sizes are 15 ply (extra small), 18 ply (small), 24 and 30 ply (medium), 42 ply (large), and 60 ply (extra large). A major U.S. wick producer says this wick is "for use in rigid dipped self-supporting candles, such as tapers."

Because these braids are flat and tensioned, the wick bends over when burned and may burn slightly off center, in the side oxidation zone of a flame.

Square Braid

These wicks look like round-cornered squares and come in various sizes with various numbering systems. One major wholesale supplier of wick uses a numbering system ranging from 6/0 (extra small) to 1/0, then beginning with #1 through #10, which  is the largest. The wicks with /0 after the number are regular braid, and the ones with the # symbol in front of the number are loosely woven, so they are fluffier and larger in diameter without actually being heavier.

This supplier recommends square-braided wicks for beeswax candles. It is my experience that a 1/0 square-braided wick is roughly equivalent to a 30-ply flat braid. Square-braided wicks tend to stand up straighter than a flat braid, burn off in the upper oxidation zone of a flame, and keep a flame centered in its candle.

As a beginning candlemaker, you will have your best success with wicks by following the instructions in the catalogs or on the packages provided by the supplier. If a wick does not burn well, use the troubleshooting guidelines offered in this bulletin (see pages 24–25), or go back to your supplier and describe what has occurred; suppliers are only too happy to answer questions.

coatings, cosmetics, industrial casting, lubricating, finishing leather and wood, and a host of other applications. Only a few of the commercially available waxes can be used in candlemaking.

Nowadays, most candles are made of paraffin or beeswax or some combination of the two. But over the centuries, candlemakers have used a wide variety of waxes. Here's a list of the traditional and modern choices for the candlemaker.

Bayberry. This wax is obtained from boiling the berries of the bayberry shrub. The wax naturally floats to the surface and is skimmed off and made into candles. Bayberries were so named because the Pilgrims first found them growing along Cape Cod Bay. But these bushes are found as far north as Nova Scotia, as far south as the Carolinas, and as far west as upstate New York. At present, bayberry wax is very expensive because the berries are not as plentiful as they were in colonial times. They are known for their sage green color and spicy aroma. Today, most bayberry candles available at a reasonable price are actually paraffin candles scented with bayberry essential oil. However, some specialty candlemaking-supply houses do offer bayberry wax.

If you wanted to create bayberry candles today, you would need 10 to 15 pounds of berries to make a pound of wax, enough for three to five pairs of dipped tapers. The berries would have to be boiled, the impurities filtered out, and the wax used for either dipping or pouring into molds.

Beeswax. Beeswax is the secretion of honeybees. They use it to build the combs where they store their honey and incubate their larvae. When bees secrete wax, they form it into the hexagonal shapes we associate with honeycombs. Amazingly, all bees, all over the world, have the ability to create hexagons with their wax — and each hexagon has angles within 3 to 4 degrees of each other! The layers of hexagons are offset from one another and result in the optimal use of space and engineered strength to allow 1 pound of hive wax to hold 22 pounds of honey! When beekeepers remove the honey for processing, they melt down the wax and sell it in blocks for cosmetics and candlemakers.

Beeswax has a wonderful sweet smell, which varies depending on the type of plants and flowers on which the bees feed. Natural beeswax is golden yellow to brownish in color, and contains bee and plant parts. It can be filtered to remove the impurities or bleached to a pure white. It is among the most desirable materials for candlemaking, as it burns slowly with a beautiful golden glow and smells sweet. It can also be mixed with paraffin to create a more affordable but long-lasting candle.

Petroleum Waxes. Paraffins are the most commonly used waxes in candlemaking. They come in a variety of melting-point ranges. Paraffin is a by-product of the process of refining crude oil into motor oil. Crude oil is distilled into fractions, or cuts, in a pipe still. Crude oil is heated at the bottom of this tall pipe and separates according to temperature into petroleum products, from heavy lubricating oil to hydrocarbon gas. Waxes from light lubricating oils are chilled and sweated or distilled off, based on their melting points. These waxes are further refined through hydrogenation and end up with very specific properties.

Generally, candlemaking paraffins are rated by melting point: low, medium, or high. Most candles require using waxes with a melting point of 125° to 150°F. When you are purchasing wax from a craft store or from a candlemaking supplier, the wax will be labeled with its melting point and intended use. Most of the time you will be adding stearic acid to the paraffin to increase its hardness and opacity.

Avoid grocery-store paraffin. The paraffin used for candles is not the same as what is sold in grocery stores for sealing jam jars. This type of paraffin has a much lower melting point than candle wax and makes very soft, drippy candles. As candlemaking is alive and growing as a do-it-yourself craft, waxes are readily available at most craft stores, even in small towns.

Synthetic Waxes. These are a class of waxes used as additives for hardening paraffin or making it pliable. Some of them are highly refined petroleum-based waxes while others are synthetic polymers that act like wax.

Tallow. There were three kinds of rendered animal fat used in candles before the 19th century — mutton fat, from sheep; beef fat; and pig fat. Of the three, mutton was considered the best and pig the worst. Mutton burned longer than the other two, tended not to smoke, and did not smell as bad. Pig, on the other hand, burned rapidly with a thick smoke and a foul smell. You may want to experiment with historical candlemaking, if only to increase your appreciation of how far the craft has come. Be sure to conduct your experiments in a well-ventilated area!

Vegetable Waxes. Candelilla and carnauba waxes are used primarily in wood and leather finishes. Candelilla is a reedlike plant, covered by waxy scales, that is native to northern Mexico and southern Texas. Carnauba is a palm grown in Brazil.

Wax Additives

There are a number of substances that can be added to wax when you want to achieve special effects in the appearance or characteristics of your candles. Here are a few of the common ones:

Microcrystallines. These are highly refined waxes that serve various purposes for the candlemaker, such as increasing layer adhesion for overdipping and increasing tackiness for wax-to-wax adhesion or modeling wax. There are two major types of micros — the soft, pliable kind, used to increase the elasticity of wax, and the hard, brittle type used to increase the durability of candles. The supplier's information will make clear what each micro is for.

Stearic Acid. While not really an acid in the caustic sense we usually associate with the term, this candlemaking essential is an animal or vegetable fat refined to a flake or powder form. Its name comes from the stear, meaning "solid fat, suet, or tallow." It is, in fact, a natural offshoot of the soapmaking craft. When fat is mixed with wood ashes (alkaline or lye), the chemical reaction produces soap and glycerin through the process of saponification. Mixing the soap with acid produces stearines. Chemical companies today still perform the same chemical reactions to produce soap, glycerin, and stearic acid from animal and vegetable fats.

Stearic acid causes two reactions when mixed with paraffin. It lowers the melting point and, when cooled, makes candles harder, which prevents bending or slumping. The reaction between wax and stearic acid is remarkable because at critical percentages and temperatures, wax and stearic acid change their individual chemical structures to become one composition. Their combination creates a hard candle with an excellent, strong crystalline structure.

Stearic acid also makes otherwise translucent paraffin more opaque. Depending on what you're trying to do, you may want to reduce or eliminate the stearic acid from certain applications, such as overdipping a layer on top of flowers when you want the flowers to show through the translucence of the natural paraffin. Stearic acid is generally sold as Triple-Pressed Stearic Acid. Do not use stearic acid with reactive metal containers or utensils, such as copper, because it is an oxidizer.

Synthetic Polymers. These are synthetic microcrystallines that serve various purposes, such as increasing luster and pliability and raising the melting point of wax. There are also various other additives that help prevent color fading and so forth.

A word of caution: Microcrystallines and polymers should not be used in percentages over 2, since they thicken wax and can cause wick problems. You may need to use a slightly larger wick if you are using high-melting-point micros. They can be used to offset the thinning effect of adding an essential oil for scent, however.

Dipping Candles

The wax formulas and wick types specified in this recipe are meant to be guidelines. The relationship among a wax's melting point, the selected wick type and size, and a finished candle's diameter is critical in determining the successful burning characteristics of a candle. Remember to take notes so that you can repeat your successes or make adjustments for your next batch of candles.

Keeping notes is very valuable and will save you lots of time in the long run. Your candlemaking notebook is an ongoing history of what worked and what didn't, if you jot down what materials and

Melting Wax

The best method for melting wax is to use a double-boiler system. Start with a heavy metal pot for the water, a smaller pot for the wax, and a trivet to hold the smaller pot off the bottom of the double boiler. Your smaller pot should be taller by at least 2 inches than the tallest candle you plan on making.

If you have a deep-fat fryer, slow-cooker, or other concealed-element heater (Crock-Pot), you can use that instead of a double boiler. The important thing is that the wax should not come into direct contact with a heat source.

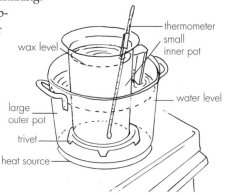

thermometer
small inner pot
wax level
water level
large outer pot
trivet
heat source

temperatures you used, and add notes later about how well the candles burned. My general rule is to write down everything I would need to know if I wanted to explain what I've done to someone else in a few weeks. What would that person want or need to know?

Materials

You will need at least 6 pounds of wax to dip three pairs of 10- by ⅞-inch tapers, more if your dipping can is very widemouthed. Only about half this wax will become candle. The rest is there only to give you the depth you need in your dipping can to completely submerge the candles. Other ingredients are:

- Wick (medium-sized, 1/0 square braid, or 30-, 36-, or 42-ply flat braid)
- One of the following wax formulas:
  - **Formula A:** 100 percent beeswax
  - **Formula B:** Paraffin with 5 to 30 percent stearic acid (I like 10 to 15 percent)
  - **Formula C:** 6 parts paraffin, 3 parts stearic acid, 1 part beeswax
  - **Formula D:** Paraffin and beeswax mixed in any pro portion (keep notes so you know what worked!)
  - **Formula E:** 60 percent paraffin, 35 percent stearic acid, 5 percent beeswax
- Color, as desired
- Scent, as desired

Equipment

Double boiler or concealed-element heater
Dipping can, at least 2 inches taller than desired length of finished candle
1 small piece of cardboard
Small weights such as washers, nuts, and curtain weights
Water bucket tall enough to submerge your entire candle
Hook or peg to hang candles on

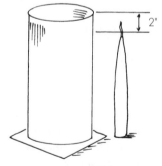

Make sure your dipping can is at least 2 inches taller than the candles you are making.

Step-by-Step

1. Measure a length of wick equal to twice the length of the desired candles plus 4 inches. For example, if you want 10-inch candles, make the wick (2 x 10) + 4 = 24 inches.

2. Tie one small weight on each end of the wick.

3. Cut a 2-inch square of cardboard. This will be your candle frame. Cut a ½-inch-deep slash on opposite sides of the cardboard. Fold the wick in half to find its center point. Align this center point with the center of the cardboard (1 inch from the edge). Push the two lengths of wick into the slashes. If you cut a 24-inch piece of wick, you will have two lengths of wick, both approximately 11 inches long, hanging from each side of the cardboard with a 1-inch space between them.

Dip the wicks into your hot wax and pull out smoothly and slowly for a good start to your dipped candles.

4. Heat the wax in double boiler or heater setup. The wax must be 10 degrees above its melting point — 155°F for medium-melting-point paraffin and stearic acid, 165°F if you used the beeswax formula. Add color and scent if desired.

5. Fill dipping can with wax to 1 inch from the top. Add wax as needed throughout the process to keep it at this height.

6. Dip the wicks down into the wax until only about 1 inch of the wicks shows below the cardboard. Hold for 30 seconds. This will allow all the air bubbles to leave the wicks. Pull the wicks up slowly and steadily when you see no more bubbles.

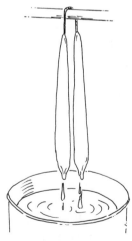

7. Hang the wicks by the cardboard on a peg or suspended dowel until wax feels cool. Do not let the wicks bend. You can

Basic tapers are repeatedly dipped in hot wax to build diameter.

speed up this cooling process by dipping the growing candles into water between each wax dip. If you decide to do this, be sure all the water droplets have come off the candles before you redip or you will have wax-covered water bubbles in your candles. These are unsightly and will cause the candles to sputter when you burn them.

8. When the wax feels cool, redip the wicks. Dip in quickly, up to the same point on the wicks as the first time, and pull out slowly and steadily. When the wax is cool, repeat this process once more. You should see a small wax buildup. If not, allow your dipping wax to cool by 5 degrees and do these two dips again.

It's a good idea to rotate your cardboard frame each time you dip to avoid bowing the candles. It also helps to be able to see the other side of the candles every other dip to be sure you are getting a smooth layering effect.

9. Continue dipping all the way up to the tip of the growing candles, cooling between dips (the cooling time will increase as the candles thicken), until the tapers are at least ¼ inch thick at their widest point. The candles will be heavy and stiff enough to weight themselves down at this point, so you can carefully slice off the bottom of each, taking the wick end and weight. The cleaner and straighter you cut the bases, the nicer your finished candle bases will be, but you can also repeat this process later in the dipping to form the finished bases.

To reuse the weights, melt off the wax by dropping into hot wax.

After the candles start to take shape, you can carefully cut off the weights.

10. Continue dipping until the candles are the desired diameter, ⅞ inch being the most common. Replenish the wax in the dipping can throughout this process as needed to maintain the depth necessary to completely submerge your candles. If the bases are elongated by drips or are uneven as you approach the finished size, trim with a knife and proceed with the last few dips. These dips will round over the bases, giving them a nice shape.

11. Some candlemakers raise the temperature of the wax to 180–200°F for the last two or three dips to improve layer adhesion. Some candlemakers use higher temperature wax, or a higher stearic acid content for the last several dips so that the candle has a harder outer coating and drips less when burned. In my experience, if you have the proper wax-to-stearic-acid ratio for the candle, this is not necessary.

12. If you want a shiny surface on your candles, dip them into cool water immediately after the last dip. Hang the candles on a hook or peg for at least an hour to cool further, then store flat and out of direct sunlight.

Troubleshooting Dipping Problems

It takes time to become a master dipper, and understanding wax temperature is probably the most crucial factor in the process. Shaping the candles and avoiding surface blemishes are also difficult. Following are a few tips for diagnosing trouble.

While Dipping

- If the candle appears to melt, the wax is too hot, or you are lingering too long in the hot wax.
- If the wax is thick and lumpy, the temperature is too cool.
- If your candle is not growing with each successive dip, the wax is too hot, or you are lingering too long in the hot wax.
- If the candle surface is blistering, the wax is too hot, or you are lingering too long in the hot wax.
- Because the wax shrinks as it cools, successive dips should be of relatively close temperatures and the candle must be cool but not cold when you redip it.

Surface Blemishes

Surface blemishes can be caused by the wax being too hot or too cold. If the wax is too hot or has too high an oil content, you may get blisters filled with air. If the wax is too cold, it will go on lumpy and thick.

Layer Adhesion

Good temperature control means good layer adhesion. Layer adhesion is the melding together of successive dips. Poor layer adhesion can result in a candle that breaks apart in concentric circles, like an onion. Good layer adhesion will produce a candle that's a solid rod of wax that will come apart only if intentionally broken.

If you are having problems with layer adhesion, try changing the following during the dipping process:

- Lengthen the submersion time.
- Shorten the time between dips.
- Raise the wax's temperature.
- Increase the ambient (room) temperature or eliminate drafts in your work area.

In fact, the four items listed above — submersion time, time between dips, wax temperature, and room temperature — are all critical. They should be recorded in your notebook and explored whenever you're having trouble dipping quality candles.

Other Dipping Projects

Once you have mastered dipping candles, you can begin to try more advanced methods of finishing your candles. From adding a color or series of colors over a white candle core, to twisting, to creating wax matches, you will learn that dipping is only the beginning.

Overdipping for Dripless Candles

If you've ever watched a commercially made, dripless candle burn, you're probably noticed that the wax on the outside of the candle melts more slowly than the wax inside. This phenomenon is caused by more than the wax's proximity to the wick. Dripless candles are often overdipped with a layer of wax with a higher melting point than the rest of the candle. This lets the wax close to the wick be consumed by the flame before it can drip.

Overdipping creates a hard outer shell on your candle. You can also use a translucent overdip to adhere decorations to the candle's surface. For this technique, use paraffin without stearic acid. You can overdip any candle you make using the same wax as the candle itself with the addition of 10 percent hardening microcrystalline. No additives are necessary for a beeswax overdip. Beeswax has a higher melting point than most paraffins, so if you want a beeswax look on a paraffin core, submerge the candle two or three times in liquid beeswax. You can overdip beeswax candles with beeswax without any problems.

Materials
- High-melting-point wax
- 5 to 30 percent stearic acid by weight (depending on technique; see above introduction)
- Cool water (optional)

Accenting the Taper

Dipping creates a natural, slim taper, but you can make this shape more pronounced. Once you've dipped the wick once, follow these instructions for the next three dips.

1. Visually split the length of the candle into quarters. Dip the candle into the wax leaving only the top quarter exposed. Cool.

2. Immerse the candle for a second dip that reaches only to the halfway point of its length. Cool.

3. Make a third dip that covers only the bottom quarter of the candle. Cool. After the above dips are made, some candlemakers make a taper dip one-third up, and then two-thirds up, to smooth over the first lines. Try this if you find your taper lines are too noticeable.

4. Continue dipping the candle (full length) until it has reached the desired diameter.

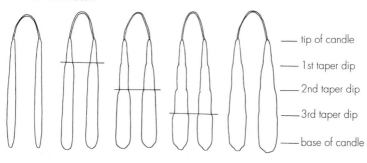

—— tip of candle

—— 1st taper dip

—— 2nd taper dip

—— 3rd taper dip

—— base of candle

Equipment
- Double boiler or concealed-element heater
- Pliers
- Bucket

Instructions

1. Melt the wax at least 20 degrees above its melting point.

2. In order to ensure good adhesion of an overdip wax, the candle should be warm, not cold. Hold it your hands until it is warm to the touch or keep it in a warm place until you are ready to dip it.

3. Holding the candle's wick with your hands or in a pair of pliers, submerge the whole candle in the overdip, then pull it out slowly and steadily. Work quickly so you don't melt the candle; be aware that it will be soft and pliable for several minutes. A second dip is not necessary but you may decide you want one to thicken the outer layer.

4. If your wax is not deep enough to submerge the whole candle, you can do half, flip it over, and do the other half. If your candle is a spiral with diagonal layers, overdip following the angle of the spiral to conceal the overlap of the overdipping.

5. For a glossy finish, plunge the candle into cool water immediately.

Overdipping an Outer Color

It is not necessary to use colored wax throughout the dipping process. A dipped (or purchased) white candle can be colored by overdipping it in one or more colors. To do this, you must have containers deep enough to submerge the candles completely — one for each color. You have to melt a large quantity of wax for each color, enough to submerge the whole candle, in the above overdipping method. There are two methods for achieving the overdip.

Method 1
1. Choose any wax formula from page 12. Melt wax either in your wax-melting pot or in individual cans for each color. Add color and scent to each can as you please. Many people use a small percentage of microcrystalline hardener in their overdip formula too.

2. Dip the whole candle, or part of it, in one color. If you want to

have two or more colors on the outside of the candle, dip the large end first, then turn the candle over and dip the tip end into a different color. By blending colors at a central band of stripes, you can create some beautiful colors on your candles.

Method 2

This alternative can be used when you have only a small quantity of a particular wax and want to use it to color a candle by overdipping.

1. Assemble deep cans for dipping — one for each color — in a double boiler or heater setup. Fill each can three-quarters full of hot (at least 150°F) water.

2. In smaller cans, combine melted wax with color. Pour the colored wax into one of the deeper cans on top of the water. Keep the water hot so the wax stays melted.

3. Dip the candle through the wax into the water. As you draw it out, the wax will adhere to the candle. You have to work fast, because the hot water will start to melt your candle.

The drawback of this method is that sometimes water adheres to the candle and is coated with wax, forming a bump on the surface of the candle.

Twisted Tapers

When you're dipping candles, you'll notice they're very pliable while warm. While they're in this pliable state, you can create some very interesting effects. I find the following twisted tapers particularly beautiful in beeswax. Dip candles as directed until they are about ½ inch at the base. Remove the cardboard spacer and twist the two candles around each other. With your fingers, form the base into a ⅞-inch stem to fit in a holder, and you have a double-wicked twisted taper. You can overdip these twisted tapers to make them look more connected. You can make braided candles the same way, using three or more candles.

Trim the base of your twisted taper and overdip if you want a more joined look.

Flattened Tapers

After dipping a taper to the desired diameter, flatten it with a rolling pin, leaving the base round so it will fit into a holder. If you grasp both ends of the still-warm candle, you can twist the flattened wax. Or you can shape a taper into leaves or petals.

Wax Matches (Vestas)

Flattened, then twisted, this taper looks quite elegant.

If you are someone who lights a lot of candles at one time and has nearly burned your fingers trying to light them before the match burns down, you need wax matches, or vestas. A vesta is a wick coated with only two or three layers of wax that can be lit and used as a long match for lighting many candles. Vestas are easy to make. Follow the basic dipping directions, but make enough wax for only three dips, using medium-sized wick.

Dipping Many Candles at Once

There are many ways to do production dipping, limited mostly by the size and shape of your dipping can or tank. In addition to the cardboard-frame technique I explained in the basic dipping instructions, there are other frames a candlemaker can use to make space between candles so they don't stick to one another. Just remember, the more apparatus you use, the more wax-coated "stuff" you will need to snip and melt off.

Any frame you use will become coated with wax that will have to be scraped or melted off. The more surfaces entering the wax, the faster the wax will be consumed, so be prepared to have more wax melted to complete the candles. Some candlemakers stop partway through the process and reclaim, by scraping, as much wax as they can to remelt for continued dipping. Depending on your frame system, this may or may not be possible.

Making Birthday Candles

These can be made in several ways. If you want, you can simply dip extra-small wick, 15 ply or smaller, the same way you do tapers. But because they are so short, you will find birthday candles are not efficiently dipped one pair at a time. Here are two other methods.

Method 1
Dip wick as if you were making a long taper (see pages 12–15). Once the candles have reached the desired diameter ($\frac{3}{16}$ inch is common), carefully snip the long candle into sections 3 $\frac{1}{4}$ inches long. Trim the wax off the top $\frac{1}{4}$ inch of each small candle to expose the wick.

Method 2
Use a shallow pan to hold the melted wax. Cut a yard of wick and draw the wick through the hot wax, from one end to the other.

Repeat the drawing process until the wax is $\frac{3}{16}$ inch thick. Allow the wax to cool a little between dips but be sure to redip while the wick is still pliable. Then snip the candles into 3$\frac{1}{4}$-inch sections as shown and trim off the top $\frac{1}{4}$ inch of wax to expose the wick.

This process, which is a variation of the drawn-candle method, can be particularly drippy, so be sure to cover your work surface and the floor with paper before beginning.

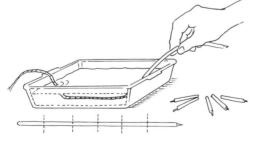

Pull a piece of wick through a tray of wax, straighten, and cut into birthday candles. For a fun variation, slightly flatten and twist before cutting.

Cleaning Up

I suggest you work on a covered surface so that wax will be caught on a disposable covering. If your candlemaking grows to the point that you have a surface just for candles, it's nice to have a smooth countertop that can be scraped clean of wax so you can save the wax for future projects.

Never, Never . . .

NEVER pour wax down the drain! It will solidify and cause you tremendous (and expensive) plumbing problems. Pour extra wax into cups or tins. After it's cooled, store the wax in plastic bags for reuse. You will be able to recycle all the wax you don't use up.

It's not a good idea to pour your double-boiler water down the drain either. Although it's mostly pure water, it probably contains some wax. You can either pour it outside, or allow it to cool thoroughly and remove the solid wax from the surface before pouring the water down the drain.

Dipping-Frame Alternatives

As you become more experienced, you might want to try other dipping methods, especially if you plan on dipping a large number of tapers.

Use hollow rods such as drinking straws and metal tubes as frame spacers and make a continuous looped wick knotted inside the tube with the spacers at the top and bottom of each planned candle.

The simplest way to dip multiple wicks is to hang or knot several wicks over a rod that can be suspended somewhere, for example between two chairs, while the candles cool. If you have a very large dipping tank, you will be able to dip an entire rod's worth of candles at once. If not, you can dip the pairs one at a time, moving the rod in and out of the wax to coat each wick.

Wax on Your Clothes

If you get wax on your clothes, you have a few options for cleanup. Try one of the following procedures.

- Wait until the wax cools; if it is sitting on the surface of the fibers, scrape it off.
- Put the cloth in the freezer and chip off the wax when it's most brittle.
- Place the cloth between layers of kraft paper and iron the wax out of the cloth and into the paper, changing the paper frequently to prevent the wax from redepositing onto the cloth.
- Boil the cloth in water, then wash and dry it. A caution here: When you pull the cloth out of the water, wax can be redeposited in a different place.
- Take the garment to a dry cleaner, letting him know you have a wax stain. Dry-cleaning solvent dissolves wax, but it's best for the cleaner to know about the wax for preliminary spot treatment.

You can buy round, metal dipping frames made to fit into some of the available round dipping cans. These have a central post with a hooked top like a coat hanger with four or more protruding rods at the top and bottom on which to thread the wicks. These are modeled after the romaine, a circular dipping system of old, used to lower wicks into cauldrons of hot wax. If you are handy with metal, you can make one of these from old coat hangers or similar-gauge wire.

If you have an oblong dipping tank, you can make a dipping frame from wood or metal, with wick wound around it and spaced properly for the size of candles you plan to make.

TROUBLESHOOTING

No matter how careful you are, you will occasionally make candles that don't come out quite right. This chart will help you identify the problem, its possible causes, and solutions.

PROBLEM	POSSIBLE CAUSES	SOLUTIONS
Lumpy	Wax too cold	Increase wax temperature
	Candle too cold when redipped	Keep candle warmer between dips; redip sooner
	Wick not fully saturated during first (priming) dip	Hold wick in wax at least 30 seconds during first dip
Wax not building up	Wax too hot	Decrease wax temperature
Blisters, surface bubbles	Candle too hot	Wait until candle cools more before redipping
	Wax too hot	Lower wax temperature
Air between layers	Wax too cool	Increase wax temperature
	Candle too cool	Keep candle warmer; redip sooner
Base of candle getting tapered	Wax too hot	Lower wax temperature
	Time in wax too long	Decrease time in wax; add more taper lines at base
Flame drowns	Wick too small to absorb and burn off enough liquid wax	Increase wick size

PROBLEM	POSSIBLE CAUSES	SOLUTIONS
Flame drowns	Wax too soft	Use wax with higher melting point or add more stearic acid
Drips	Burning in draft	Shelter candle from drafts
	Wax too soft	Use harder wax; overdip with harder wax
	Wick too small	Use larger wick
Flame sputters	Water in wax or wick	Make sure no water droplets remain on candle cooled by dipping in water
Smokes	Burning in draft	Shelter from drafts
	Wick too large; consumes wax faster than it can melt	Use smaller wick
Won't stay lit	Wick too small to melt enough wax to fuel	Use larger wick
	Wax too hard for wick to melt	Use softer wax
Small flame	Wax too hard	Use softer wax
	Wick too small	Use larger wick
	Wick clogged with pigment	Use oil-soluble dyes
Wick burns hole only down candle center	Wick too small	Use larger wick
	Wax too hard	Use softer wax
Flame too large	Wick too large	Use smaller wick

Safety Equipment and Procedures

The importance of safety in candlemaking cannot be overstated. You must be aware of this fact at all times: Making candles requires the use of flammable materials around a heat source. Avoid working around open flames unless it is absolutely necessary.

Always heat wax in a double boiler or in a heating vessel with encased elements. When using a double boiler, never let the water boil away. Replenish the water frequently to maintain the proper level.

Never leave burning candles unattended.

Keep these items handy for extinguishing a fire, and know how to use them:

- Fire extinguisher (ABC type)
- Metal pan lid to starve a fire of oxygen
- Baking soda to smother flames
- A damp cloth or towel

If a fire starts while you are making candles, turn off the source of heat and use an extinguisher, pan lid, baking soda, or damp towel to deplete the oxygen level available to the fire and smother it.

Never use water to extinguish a wax fire! This can cause wax to splatter and increase your chances of being burned.

Splattering on Skin

If you splatter yourself or even accidentally dip a finger into hot paraffin, it probably won't burn you severely, but it's wise to have cold water nearby so that you can submerge your skin until the wax is cool enough to remove. Paraffin will cool and chip off, but the stickiness of beeswax prevents chipping. The heat of the wax will continue to burn until the wax is removed or completely cooled.

Decorating Your Candles with Wax

There are a variety of ways you can use special wax techniques for colors to put finishing touches on your candles. You can create candles unlike anyone else's or duplicate beautiful centerpieces you've seen elsewhere.

Warm the Wax

Before you begin decorating candles, be sure they are warm. They should be at least 85°F, warmer if possible. When I'm decorating my candles, I keep them near the woodstove or heater. In candle factories, they have a "warm room" set up with heaters and temperature controls to keep the wax at a constant 85 to 90°F.

Decorative Overdipping

Overdipping lends itself to several decorative techniques in candlemaking. You can color the outside of a white candle, create a series of colored stripes or ripples, refresh a faded candle, or attach decorations.

Creating Stripes. To make a simple stripe design with overdipping, wrap pieces of masking tape around the places on a candle where you do not want a stripe. For example, if you have a plain white candle that you want to stripe with dark blue, apply the tape everywhere you want to maintain the candle's original white color. Now overdip it in colored wax, let it cool, and carefully remove the tape. To make stripes without masking tape, dip a white candle in one color (red) from its bottom to its halfway point. Turn the candle over and immerse it in a second color (yellow) from its top to a point where it overlaps the first color at least an inch. This overlap will produce a stripe of a third color, in this case orange.

Decorating with Sheet Wax

Decorating Wax is smooth-surfaced sheets designed to be cut into shapes and stuck onto candles. You can buy a pack with 22 different colors to play with. In addition to making one-of-a-kind shapes or figures to decorate your candles, you can also try the millefiori technique.

Millefiori, which means "thousand flowers," is a technique used throughout history by glassmakers. The round, flowerlike motifs are created by making logs, or canes, out of glass, or, in this case, wax. When the log is sliced, each slice is a duplicate of the same design. These slices can be used as a repeat pattern on the surface of a candle. You can press the shapes onto your warmed candle.

Flower, Leaf, and Herb Appliqué

You can attach relatively flat bits of plants and natural fibers to candles with variations of the overdipping technique. These can be pressed flowers and herbs or freshly dried materials. Do not use stearic acid in the wax, as it will make the overdip opaque and obscure your decorations.

Remember, when decorating your candles, flammable surface treatments can be dangerous! These materials must be used with caution. I've seen dried flower petals on a candle surface catch fire. This form of decoration is best used on larger-diameter candles where the wax pool will be contained and the surface will remain relatively unmelted. Never leave a burning candle of any type unattended.

Begin by attaching the plant or fiber decorations by one of the following methods:

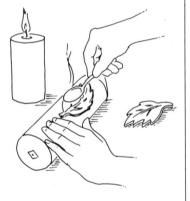

- Pin the flowers to the surface of the candle with straight pins.
- Dip the plant material in melted wax and then attach it to the candle while it is still hot.
- Heat the back of a spoon or use a heat pen to warm the surface of the candle, and then adhere the plant parts to the softened wax.

Once the plant material is adhered to the candle, overdip the entire candle in clear wax. Be sure to pull it out of the overdip slowly, particularly as the decorations emerge, to prevent wax from dripping down the sides.

While the overdip wax is still hot, carefully push on all the tips and corners of the leaves and flowers so they are fully adhered to the candle's surface. Remove the pins. Overdip again to cover any prints and pinholes, then plunge the candle into cool water for a shiny surface.

Candle Storage Tips

- Candles must be stored flat. This is particularly true of long tapers, which tend to bend if airspace is left beneath them.
- Store candles in a place that stays cool and dark year-round. Temperatures above 70°F for prolonged periods of time can soften the candles, which can bend or even stick together at these high temperatures. But if they are wrapped and stored properly, your candles should be able to withstand summertime heat.
- Do not refrigerate or freeze candles. This can cause them to crack!
- Candle colors may fade if continuously exposed to light, so be sure to cover the box or close the drawer or cabinet where you store your candles.
- Candle scents can dissipate if the candles are not wrapped in an impermeable covering such as plastic.

Decorative Candle Wrapping

Candles make wonderful gifts, whether or not you make them yourself. They are a great addition to gift baskets because they add color and texture, and because they're useful.

Tissue Paper

For a single candle, simply roll tissue paper securely around it and tape or tie with ribbon. To wrap pairs or multiple candles, roll the paper completely around the first candle, then insert the second one so that it does not touch the first and continue rolling. This way, the candles are separated from each other by a layer of paper and serve as stiffeners for each other.

Fabric and Ribbon

For gift-giving, I like to wrap the bottom half of a candle in fabric or interesting paper tied with a bow. This allows the top half of the candle to be exposed so people can see, feel, and smell it. If necessary, add a piece of cardboard for extra stiffness before wrapping. This method works best for undecorated candles, since the fabric wrap might cover or clash with the design of the candle.

Suppliers

There are many craft suppliers who sell candlemaking materials. I suggest you try to find the ones in your area, as wax is heavy and costly to ship. There are also mail-order suppliers who carry a more complete or specialized lines of candlemaking materials, and I have compiled a list of some of them here.

In my experience, candlemakers are happy to share information, and so are these suppliers. Your success can only serve to contribute to theirs, so don't be afraid to ask questions.

Aztec International, Inc.
800-369-5357
www.candlemaking.com

Betterbee
800-632-3379
www.betterbee.com

Bitter Creek Candle Supply
877-635-8929
www.candlesupply.com

CandleChem Company
508-586-1880
www.candlechem.com

The Candlemaker
888-251-4618
www.thecandlemaker.com

Candle Maker's Supplies
mail@candlemakers.co.uk
www.candlemakers.co.uk

The Candlewic Company
800-368-3352
www.candlewic.com

Dadant & Sons, Inc.
888-922-1293
www.dadant.com

Earth Guild
800-327-8448
www.earthguild.com

GloryBee Foods, Inc.
800-456-7923
www.glorybee.com

SpiritCrafts
866-992-2635
www.spiritcrafts.net

Yaley Enterprises
800-959-2539
www.yaley.com

Other Storey Titles You Will Enjoy

The Candlemaker's Companion, by Betty Oppenheimer.
Roll, pour, mold, and dip for every occasion with these
comprehensive wax-to-wick instructions.
208 pages. Paper. ISBN 978-1-58017-366-7.

Making Transparent Soap, by Catherine Failor.
Step-by-step directions to produce transparent
soaps that are mild, rich, and creamy.
144 pages. Paper. ISBN 978-1-58017-244-8.

Melt & Mold Soap Crafting, by C. Kaila Westerman.
Colorful, eye-catching soaps, made in the microwave
without lye or other hazardous chemicals.
144 pages. Paper. ISBN 978-1-58017-293-6.

Milk-Based Soaps, by Casey Makela.
Extensive coverage of the processes of making milk-based soaps,
long recognized for their gentleness and beautifying effects.
112 pages. Paper. ISBN 978-0-88266-984-7.

**The Natural Soap Book: Making Herbal
and Vegetable-Based Soaps,** by Susan Miller Cavitch.
Basic recipes for soaps made without chemical additives
and synthetic ingredients, as well as ideas on scenting,
coloring, cutting, trimming, and wrapping soaps.
192 pages. Paper. ISBN 978-0-88266-888-8.

The Soapmaker's Companion, by Susan Miller Cavitch.
A resource for beginner and advanced soapmakers alike, from
mastering basic skills to creating soaps with a personal touch.
288 pages. Paper. ISBN 978-0-88266-965-6.

Trash-to-Treasure Papermaking, by Arnold E. Grummer.
Dozens of fabulous techniques and projects to transform any paper
at hand — from wrapping paper to junk mail — into beautiful
handmade paper.
208 pages. Paper. ISBN 978-1-60342-547-6.

These and other books from Storey Publishing are available
wherever quality books are sold or by calling 1-800-441-5700.
Visit us at *www.storey.com* or sign up for our newsletter
at *www.storey.com/signup*.